ICEL

TRAVEL GUIDE

A Definitive Itinerary Companion to Unveiling the Hidden Gems and Must-See Attraction Sites in the Land of Fire and Ice.

2023

Patricia J. Parks

COPYRIGHT

Patricia J. Parks

TABLE OF CONTENTS

INTRODUCTION

Overview of Iceland

The fascinating Nordic island nation of Iceland sometimes referred to as the "Land of Fire and Ice," is situated in the North Atlantic Ocean. It is well known for its breathtaking natural features, which include volcanoes, glaciers, hot springs, waterfalls, and geothermal zones.

Despite its name, Iceland has a milder climate than one might anticipate, due to the Gulf Stream's warming effect. The nation entices visitors with a distinctive combination of natural beauty, lively culture, and gracious hospitality.

Iceland, which has a population of about 360,000 and a geographic area of over 103,000 square kilometres, is one of the least populous nations in Europe. The capital city of Reykjavik and its surrounding environs are home to the vast majority of Icelanders. Despite having a tiny population, Iceland has made strides in the fields of gender equality, environmental sustainability, and renewable energy.

Geography And Climate

The geography of Iceland is distinguished by a wide variety of landscapes that have been formed by glacial and volcanic activity. The Mid-Atlantic Ridge, a tectonic border where the Eurasian and North American plates collide, is where the island is located. Iceland is a geologically active and dynamic place because of the numerous volcanoes, geothermal hotspots, and geysers that are produced by this geological phenomenon.

In the southeast of the nation stands Vatnajökull, the biggest glacier in all of Europe. Icebergs, ice caves, and glacial lagoons are some of the fascinating elements that make up this frozen world.

Additionally, Iceland is home to several waterfalls that display the nation's unadulterated natural beauty, including the famous Gullfoss, Seljalandsfoss, and Skógafoss.

Iceland has a subarctic climate with warm summers and milder-than-average winters given its high latitude. Average summer temperatures range from 10 to 15 degrees Celsius (50 to 59 degrees Fahrenheit) due to the moderate effect of the Gulf Stream. The average winter temperature is approximately 0 degrees Celsius (32 degrees Fahrenheit), which is milder than anticipated.

It's important to remember that weather may be unexpected, so travellers should be ready for sudden shifts and a variety of situations along the way.

Culture and History

Over a thousand years ago, Iceland began to develop a rich and captivating history. Norse Vikings who were led by people like Ingólfur Arnarson and his family settled the nation in the ninth century. Iceland's early history and colonisation are well-documented in the mediaeval Icelandic Sagas, which were written during the 12th and 14th centuries.

Iceland has endured isolation, independence wars, and economic hardships over the ages. But the nation has now established itself as an affluent and progressive one. Since gaining its independence from Denmark in 1944, Iceland has flourished, rising to the top of the global development and progress rankings.

Icelandic mythology, sagas, and Viking ancestry are fundamental to the country's culture. The nation takes great pleasure in upholding its cultural customs, such as the observance of the midwinter festival known as Orrablót and the survival of the Icelandic language, which still has striking resemblances to Old Norse.

Icelandic culture places a high value on the arts and literature, and it has a large population of published authors. The capital, Reykjavik, is known for having a thriving cultural culture and hosts several festivals and events all year long. Icelandic music, which includes traditional folk songs as well as modern artists like Björk and Sigur Rós, has achieved international success and improved the prestige of the nation's culture.

Language & Currency

Icelandic, a dialect of North Germanic that is closely linked to Old Norse, is the official language of Iceland. Even though the majority of Icelanders are competent in English, especially in tourist regions, it is always appreciated when tourists make an effort to acquire a few fundamental Icelandic words. The syntax and pronunciation of the language are notoriously difficult, although locals are typically glad to assist visitors in navigating the linguistic complexities.

Iceland uses the Icelandic Króna (ISK) as its official currency. Although most businesses take credit cards, it is still a good idea to have some cash on hand for smaller stores or rural locations where card payment may not be an option. Major towns and cities have plenty of ATMs, making it simple to get cash.

As you set off on your Icelandic journey, bear in mind that having a basic awareness of the country's history, geography, climate, culture, language, and financial system will improve your travels and help you develop closer ties with the amazing land and its people.

As you prepare to immerse yourself in the stunning scenery, intriguing history, and distinctive cultural experiences that this wonderful nation has to offer, keep in mind to pack appropriately for Iceland's varied weather conditions.

PLANNING YOUR TRIP

The Best Time to Go

Your tastes and the activities you want to engage in will determine the ideal time to visit Iceland. Iceland has four different seasons, each with its own set of experiences and natural occurrences.

Summer (Jun to Aug): This is the busiest travel period in Iceland. The weather is often pleasant at this time of year, with typical highs and lows between 10 and 15 degrees Celsius (50 and 59 degrees Fahrenheit). The length of the days and the occurrence of the Midnight Sun phenomena result in nearly 24 hours of daylight. The stunning landscapes of Iceland are best explored during the summer, along with hiking, camping, and other outdoor pursuits. It's also a perfect time to see the unique wildlife of the nation, such as puffins and whales.

Fall (Sept to Nov): Iceland's landscapes display breathtaking autumnal hues during Fall. The temperature drops and the people start to thin out. Since the trails are still open and the fall foliage gives the landscape a special touch, September is a great month for hiking. Additionally, as the evenings get darker in the fall, it's a great time to see the Northern Lights.

Winter (Dec. to Feb.): Iceland can be visited at any time of year, but winter is particularly alluring for those looking for the captivating beauty of snow-covered landscapes and the chance to experience the Northern Lights. Wintertime temperatures vary from 30 to 41 degrees Fahrenheit to -1 to 5 degrees Celsius. This is a popular period for winter sports including snowmobile, glacier treks, and ice cave exploring. There are just a few hours of daylight each day, which is a crucial fact to keep in mind.

Spring (March to May): In Iceland, Spring season is one of transition. The landscapes come alive with vivid colours as the snow starts to melt. Compared to summer, spring provides a calmer and more affordable experience. Given that the migratory birds are about to arrive and the waterfalls are in full flow, it is a fantastic time for photographers.

Visa Requirements & Travel Documents

It's crucial to comprehend the visa requirements and have all relevant travel paperwork in order before visiting Iceland. Iceland is a part of the Schengen Area, which permits travellers from specific nations to enter visa-free for brief visits.

With a current passport or national identity card, citizens of the European Union (EU), European Economic Area (EEA), or Switzerland may enter Iceland. To find out if they need a visa, residents of non-EU/EEA nations should visit the website of the Icelandic Directorate of Immigration or speak with their regional embassy or consulate of Iceland.

The application procedure for nationals of nations requiring a visa normally includes submitting an application form, a valid passport with a certain validity term, proof of travel insurance, proof of lodging, and adequate financial resources to sustain your stay. Applying for a visa well in advance of your intended trip is advised.

Getting to Iceland

Keflavik International Airport (KEF), which is about 50 kilometres (31 miles) southwest of Reykjavik, is the airport that serves Iceland's capital city. The main international entry point for Iceland is Keflavik Airport, which provides direct flights from many significant cities in Europe, North America, and other areas of the world.

Regular flights to and from Iceland are run by several carriers, notably WOW Air and Icelandair. To get the greatest bargains, it is advised to compare flight costs and make reservations in advance. Flight times vary based on the point of departure; flights leaving from North America normally last 5 to 7 hours.

Transportation within Iceland

There are several ways to get about Iceland after you are there, including:

Renting a Car: You can explore Iceland at your speed and with more flexibility if you rent a car. Both at Keflavik Airport and downtown Reykjavik, there are several automobile rental agencies in operation. It's crucial to reserve your car in advance, especially during the busiest summer months when space may be scarce. Remember that driving in Iceland may be difficult, especially in the winter, so it's important to become familiar with the local driving laws and weather patterns.

Public Transportation: Major cities and tourist hotspots are connected by an extensive bus network in Iceland. Everywhere in the nation, regular routes are run by the major bus company, Straetó. The bus service, however, could be less frequent in rural regions or during the winter. It's a good idea to research bus timetables beforehand and adjust your travel plans appropriately.

Guided Tours: Joining guided tours is a popular way to see Iceland, particularly for tourists who don't want to drive or who want the knowledge of a local guide. The Golden Circle, the South Coast, and the Highlands are just a few of the well-known locations that are covered by a variety of tour companies' extensive selection of alternatives, which vary from day trips to multi-day excursions.

Domestic Flights: Domestic flights offer a practical choice for travelling across Iceland if you have limited time or intend to visit isolated areas. Destinations all around the nation are served by domestic airports like Reykjavik Domestic Airport (RKV). Domestic flights are offered by carriers including Eagle Air and Air Iceland Connect. It's crucial to keep in mind that there can be luggage limitations on domestic flights, so make sure to check with the airline before your journey.

Accommodation Options

Iceland provides a variety of lodging choices to accommodate different tastes and price ranges:

Hotels: There are many hotels available in Reykjavik and other major Icelandic cities, ranging from low-cost accommodations to five-star hotels. It is important to reserve lodging in advance, especially during the busiest times of the year when space may be scarce. Because there may be fewer hotels available in rural places, think about other lodging possibilities.

Guesthouses & Farm Stays: These accommodations provide a singular chance to experience Icelandic hospitality and get fully immersed in the community. These lodgings frequently have a homey ambiance and are maintained by families. They may be discovered all around Iceland, both in remote spots and on well-travelled paths.

Camping: There are many campgrounds spread out over Iceland, making it a haven for campers. Camping is a more cost-effective choice that brings you closer to nature. Toilets, showers, and kitchen facilities are frequently available at campgrounds. It's crucial to be ready for shifting weather patterns and to confirm whether camping is permitted in a particular location as some may want permits.

Hostels: For visitors on a tight budget and those seeking to connect with like-minded explorers, hostels are a popular option. Numerous hostels with shared dorm rooms or individual rooms are available in Reykjavik and other significant towns. Common kitchens and gathering spaces are frequently offered by hostels, fostering a lively atmosphere.

Unique Accommodations: Iceland also provides distinctive lodging choices, like glass igloos, eco-friendly lodges, and ice hotels. These experiences are frequently found in picturesque and far-flung areas, and they offer an unforgettable stay. Due to the great demand for these lodgings, making reservations in advance is advised.

Packing Essentials

It's crucial to pack for a variety of weather scenarios and outdoor activities while going to Iceland. Here are some necessities to think about:

Clothing: In Iceland, layering is essential. Include a high-quality waterproof jacket and pants on your list of warm, windproof, and waterproof apparel to bring. Bring warm, waterproof hiking boots, fleece or wool sweaters, and thermal base layers. To stay comfortable in cooler weather, don't forget to carry thermal socks, scarves, gloves, and caps.

Outdoor Gear: Bring a reliable backpack, a reusable water bottle, a headlamp, and a compass or GPS if you intend to explore Iceland's natural beauties. Since the sun may be harsh even during the cooler months, wearing sunglasses and sunscreen are also necessary.

Electronics and Chargers: Iceland uses the Europlug (Type C and F) standard for power outlets, therefore if your electronics require a different plug type, pack an adapter. For extended outdoor activities, consider bringing a power bank, and don't forget to carry chargers for your gadgets.

Toiletries & Medications: Bring your regular toiletries and any essential prescription drugs, as well as your customary toiletries. A small first-aid kit, bug repellent, and other personal care products you may need are also smart additions.

Travel Essentials: Don't forget to pack your passport, proof of travel insurance, and any required visas. Keep duplicates of crucial papers like your passport and trip schedule in both hard copy and digital form. Other useful items to bring are a portable phone charger, a reusable water bottle, and a trip guide or maps.

Photography Equipment: There are several possibilities to take beautiful pictures in Iceland. To record the grandeur of the surroundings, think about bringing a

DSLR or mirrorless camera along with additional memory cards, batteries, and a tripod.

You'll be well-prepared to enjoy your Icelandic adventure if you properly plan your trip and carry the necessary supplies. The right planning and a sense of anticipation for the delights that await you will enhance your trip, whether you're exploring glaciers, searching for waterfalls, or relaxing in hot springs.

EXPLORING REYKJAVIK

Overview of Reykjavik

The dynamic and picturesque capital of Iceland, Reykjavik, is a place that combines urban delights with natural beauty and provides a variety of cultural events. Reykjavik, while small, has a vibrant environment and a vibrant cultural scene that draws tourists from all over the world.

Reykjavik, which was founded in the ninth century, is renowned for its vibrant homes, cutting-edge construction, and breathtaking vistas of the nearby mountains and the North Atlantic Ocean. Because of its small size and pleasant environment, the city is attractive and simple to navigate on foot.

Must See Attractions in Reykjavik

A variety of attractions are available in Reykjavik that highlight the city's distinct personality and Icelandic heritage. The following are some popular sights to see:

Hallgrímskirkja: A tall church that dominates the skyline of the city, Hallgrímskirkja is one of Reykjavik's most recognizable sights. From its observation deck, the building's unusual style, which drew inspiration from Icelandic nature, offers breathtaking panoramic views of Reykjavik.

Harpa Concert Hall: A spectacular, contemporary performance venue situated by the waterfront that is renowned for its avant-garde design. Numerous cultural events, including concerts, plays, and exhibits, are held there. A photographer's dream, the building's glass front makes lovely reflections and interacts with natural light.

Sun Voyager: The Sun Voyager, a well-known sculpture near Reykjavik's waterfront, is a magnificent work of art that embodies the spirit of exploration and adventure. It provides a wonderful location for a stroll in the park and a superb vantage point for taking in the natural beauty of the area.

Reykjavik City Pond and Tjörnin: This picturesque lake in the middle of the city is a favourite destination for both locals and tourists. It is home to a variety of bird species. It frequently freezes over in the winter, providing a magnificent backdrop for ice skating or just taking a quiet stroll.

Perlan: A distinctive landmark that is home to exhibition rooms, a café, and an observation deck. It is located on Öskjuhlíð Hill. It provides sweeping views of Reykjavik and has recurring exhibits that shed light on Iceland's cultural history and natural beauty.

Museums & Art Galleries

There are several museums and galleries in Reykjavik that provide an insight into Iceland's history, art, and traditions. Reykjavik also has a thriving arts and cultural scene. Listed below are a few prominent businesses:

National Museum of Iceland: Situated in the centre of Reykjavik, offers a thorough overview of Iceland's history from the country's colonisation to the present. Its relics, archaeological discoveries, and engaging exhibits bring the nation's past to life.

Reykjavik Art Museum: Consisting of three separate locations, exhibits a wide variety of contemporary and modern Icelandic art. The museum offers changing exhibits, artist lectures, and educational events throughout its many spaces.

The Settlement Exhibition: A museum offering a distinctive experience that transports visitors to the Viking Age, is located in the heart of Reykjavik. It displays the Viking longhouse ruins that were found during excavations, shedding light on Iceland's early habitation.

Árbær Open Air Museum: Situated outside of Reykjavik, Rbr Open Air Museum gives visitors a look at Iceland's rural past. It offers an interactive experience where visitors can learn about Icelandic culture and traditions and exhibits wonderfully maintained old structures, including conventional turf cottages.

Shopping & Dining

From upscale shops to neighbourhood markets, Reykjavik provides a wide variety of shopping alternatives where you may purchase distinctive Icelandic goods and gifts. The city's main retail strip, Laugavegur, is dotted with boutiques, cafes, and eateries, making for a lively and diverse shopping experience.

Icelandic Design: Reykjavik is a centre for Icelandic design, which is renowned for its ingenuity and workmanship. Look through neighbourhood boutiques and concept stores to find clothing, jewellery, home décor, and artwork that capture Iceland's distinctive look.

Kolaportið Flea Market: Kolaportiðis a lively marketplace where you may find a variety of things, including antique clothes, books, vinyl records, and traditional Icelandic cuisine items. It is situated beside the ancient harbour.

Food Markets: Reykjavik has a vibrant food culture, so stopping by one is a fantastic chance to try some regional specialties. The Hlemmur Mathöll dining hall and the Reykjavík Flea Market are well-known places to sample handcrafted goods, fresh fish, and traditional Icelandic fare.

Reykjavik has a wide variety of dining establishments to suit all tastes. The city is a gastronomic mecca, with inventive Icelandic food and cuisines from throughout the world. All across the city are eateries, cafés, and bistros that provide a variety of options to satisfy all tastes and dietary requirements. Don't pass up the chance to sample Icelandic delicacies like raw fish, Icelandic lamb, and skyr, a traditional dairy delicacy that is similar to yoghurt.

Nightlife in Reykjavik

The nightlife in Reykjavik is thriving and well-known for its upbeat vibe. Evenings in the city are lively, with a variety of bars, clubs, and live music places to pick from. Here are some well-liked locations and businesses for a wonderful night out:

Laugavegur and Austurstræti: These are well-known areas for Reykjavik's nightlife and they are lined with pubs and clubs. There are places for everyone, from quaint pubs to hip cocktail bars. Popular nightclub Austur is renowned for its energetic dance floors and live music performances.

Harpa Concert Hall: Harpa is a centre for nightlife in addition to being a cultural facility. It offers a distinctive and unforgettable evening experience by hosting a variety of events, such as concerts, DJ sets, and shows.

Microbreweries and Craft Beer Bars: Reykjavik is home to several microbreweries and craft beer bars. Iceland boasts a vibrant craft beer culture. Explore the city's beer scene while consuming locally made beers, which frequently feature distinctive Icelandic ingredients.

Live Music: With a wide variety of live music venues featuring both local and international talent, Reykjavik is renowned for its vibrant music scene. You may discover a wide variety of genres and performances to fit your musical taste, from small pubs to major concert venues.

It's crucial to remember that Reykjavik's nightlife may be exciting, especially on weekends and during the summer. Be ready for late evenings and make sure to educate yourself with regional traditions and laws about safe drinking and alcohol usage.

Discovering Reykjavik provides a great array of creative interactions, gastronomic pleasures, cultural adventures, and buzzing nightlife. Due to the city's small size and straightforward navigation, you may readily immerse yourself in its distinct charm and learn about the core of Icelandic culture. Reykjavik is certain to enchant and leave enduring impressions thanks to its famous monuments and secret jewels.

GOLDEN CIRCLE ROUTE

One of Iceland's most well-known tourist itineraries, the Golden Circle offers an enthralling journey around some of the nation's most outstanding natural and historical monuments. This chapter discusses the main attractions along the Golden Circle route so you may fully appreciate Iceland's breathtaking scenery and rich cultural heritage.

Þingvellir National Park

The starting point of the Golden Circle path is Þingvellir National Park, a UNESCO World Heritage site. This geologically significant region, which is around 40 kilometres east of Reykjavik, is a must-see location.

Historical Significance: Þingvellir is well-known for being the location of the Alingi, the first parliament in history, which was founded in 930 AD. It offered a venue for debates, legislation, and conflicts and functioned as the nation's chieftains' gathering place. You may follow in the early settlers' footsteps and see the cradle of democracy by exploring the park.

Geological Marvel: Þingvellir is a special geological location since it is situated in the rift valley between the North American and Eurasian tectonic plates. The park provides access to the Almannagjá fissure, where the two continents are gradually drifting apart. You can also be in awe of the Silfra fissure, which is renowned for its pristine waters and offers a once-in-a-lifetime chance to snorkel or dive between the continents.

Natural Beauty: With breathtaking vistas that display Iceland's untainted and unadulterated beauty, Þingvellir National Park is a visual feast. The park is home to expansive lava fields, breathtaking cliffs, and tranquil lakes like Þingvallatn, the biggest natural lake in the nation. You may explore the park's unique flora and wildlife while taking in the peace of the surroundings on hiking routes.

Geysir Geothermal Area

A geothermal paradise that displays the ferocious powers of nature at work is the Geysir Geothermal Area. This region, which is roughly Þingvellir, is home to several geysers and hot springs, including the well-known Strokkur geyser.

Strokkur Geyser: The main attraction of the Geysir Geothermal Area is the Strokkur. Every 5 to 10 minutes, this geyser bursts, spewing scorching water up to 40 metres into the air. It is very amazing to experience Strokkur's eruptions in all their strength and beauty.

Geysir: Even though the original Geysir, from which all geysers take their name, is presently inactive, it nonetheless has historical value as one of the first recognized geysers. Even if it doesn't often erupt these days, Strokkur, its neighbour, more than makes up for it.

Hot Springs & Mud Pools: The Geysir Geothermal Area is peppered with hot springs and boiling mud pools, which together create an exotic and strange environment. There are countless options for photography and exploring because of the vivid colours and flowing steam.

Geothermal Power: Iceland's use of geothermal energy is best demonstrated by the Geysir Geothermal Area. A sizable amount of Iceland's electricity and hot water is generated by the region's geothermal power plants, demonstrating the nation's dedication to renewable energy sources.

Gullfoss Waterfall

One of Iceland's most recognizable natural beauties, Gullfoss Waterfall, may be found by continuing around the Golden Circle. Gullfoss, a magnificent cascade that can be seen in the Hvtá River canyon, will wow you with its strength and beauty.

Magnificent Waterfall: Gullfoss, which translates to "Golden Falls," plunges in two parts, producing an enthralling scene. The top falls plunge around 11 metres into the rough canyon below, then plunge another 21 metres. The sheer amount of water is breathtaking, especially in the summer when glacier melt is at its greatest.

Surrounding Scenery: Gullfoss is made more alluring by the area's scenery. The waterfall's mist and rainbows on bright days provide a magical element to the image, which is set against the majestic canyon cliffs. Being in the mist may lead to interesting picture possibilities, so be ready with waterproof equipment to get the best photograph.

History & Conservation: The history of Gullfoss' preservation is extensive. Early in the 20th century, the waterfall was spared from potential hydropower construction because of the efforts of a local environmentalist named Sigrur Tómasdóttir. Gullfoss is still a representation of Iceland's dedication to protecting its natural resources and is today preserved as a national monument.

Other Attractions Along the Route

Beyond its three primary attractions, the Golden Circle path has other attractions. Between the major sites, you'll pass through more noteworthy sights and activities that deepen your journey:

Faxi Waterfall: Along the Golden Circle path, there is a less well-known waterfall called Faxi, which is also known as Vatnsleysufoss. In contrast to Gullfoss, this charming cascade is surrounded by beautiful scenery and offers a calmer, more personal experience.

Friðheimar Tomato Farm: It is a distinctive tomato farm that offers a fascinating look into Icelandic agriculture. It is close to the Geysir Geothermal Area. Visit the greenhouse, discover the cutting-edge methods employed for year-round tomato growth, and have lunch at the charming farm café.

Secret Lagoon: The Secret Lagoon (Gamla Laugin) is a well-kept secret that is well worth exploring if you need a moment of relaxation. This natural geothermal hot spring, which is close to the settlement of Flir, offers a serene and genuine bathing experience while being surrounded by steaming scenery and an unspoiled environment.

Kerið Crater: Kerið is a volcanic crater with brilliant blue water that may be reached by taking a little diversion off the Golden Circle road. The chance to enter the crater and stroll around its rim while observing the striking colours and geological structures is provided by this natural wonder.

A fascinating overview of Iceland's natural beauty, historical importance, and geothermal marvels can be found along the Golden Circle path. Each stop along the way offers a remarkable experience, from the historically significant grounds of Þingvellir National Park to the exploding geysers at Geysir and the breathtaking grandeur of Gullfoss Waterfall. The journey is further enhanced along the route by lesser-known attractions and undiscovered treasures, making the Golden Circle a wonderful excursion in the country of fire and ice.

SOUTH COAST ADVENTURE

A location of unmatched natural beauty, Iceland's south coast is home to impressive waterfalls, gorgeous black sand beaches, glacial lagoons, and sizable national parks. This chapter provides an exciting tour through some of Iceland's most alluring landscapes as it covers the South Coast's major landmarks.

Seljalandsfoss Waterfall

Seljalandsfoss is a captivating waterfall that distinguishes out for having a special feature: a tunnel that allows tourists to wander below the cascade's rushing water. Seljalandsfoss is a must-see attraction on the South Coast and is situated along the Ring Road around 120 kilometres east of Reykjavik.

Walk Behind the Falls: It's an immersive experience to be able to go behind the curtain of flowing water. Be prepared with suitable footwear and weather gear since the path may be slick. Feel the mist on your face as you take in the stunning view of the surroundings from a different angle.

Panoramic View: Seljalandsfoss provides spectacular panoramas over the Icelandic landscape. Views of the surrounding Eyjafjallajökull volcano, green farms, and undulating hills may be seen from the top of the waterfall. A picture-perfect image is created by the tumbling water and the lovely surroundings.

Photography Opportunities: Seljalandsfoss is a favourite location for photographers, particularly at sunrise and sunset, when the light is at its most beautiful. Capture the waterfall's ethereal beauty against the many hues of the sky, or try long exposure photography to get ethereal, smooth water effects.

Skógafoss Waterfall

Another well-known waterfall on the South Coast is Skógafoss, which is renowned for its imposing height and overwhelming force. This magnificent waterfall, which can be found near the hamlet of Skógar, some 30 kilometres east of Seljalandsfoss, is an absolute must-see on any South Coast excursion.

Magnificent Cascade: Skógafoss drops around 60 metres into a tranquil lake below, producing a stunning display of water and mist. Visitors are mesmerised by the waterfall's magnificence due to its tremendous force and thunderous roar.

Rainbows and Myths: On bright days, the mist from Skógafoss frequently produces vivid rainbows, giving the area a mystical touch. Folklore in the area claims that anybody bold enough to enter the mist will find a treasure chest concealed below the waterfall.

Hiking Opportunities: The renowned Fimmvöruháls hiking trail begins in Skógafoss and leads to the breathtaking órsmörk Nature Reserve. The path offers an exciting multi-day trip as it leads you through a variety of scenery, including lush valleys, lava fields, and volcanic craters.

Reynisfjara Black Sand Beach

About 180 kilometres east of Reykjavik, in the vicinity of the settlement of Vk Mrdal, is the captivating black sand beach known as Reynisfjara. Reynisfjara, an alluring location that displays the unadulterated beauty of Iceland's shoreline, is distinguished by its distinctive geological characteristics and strong waves.

Basalt Column Cave: The Hálsanefshellir basalt column cave is one of Reynisfjara's most stunning features. These volcanic hexagonal basalt columns have an alien feel to them and provide a beautiful backdrop for photographs.

Reynisdrangar Sea Stacks: The Reynisdrangar Sea Stacks rise from the water right off the coast of Reynisfjara. These imposing rock formations provide a mesmerising silhouette against the rushing waves, adding to the beach's dramatic appeal. These piles were once living trolls who were turned to stone, according to Icelandic tradition.

Powerful Waves: Use caution when visiting the beach at Reynisfjara because the waves may be quite strong and unexpected. Keep a safe distance from the water's edge and pay alert to any warning indications. It's humbling to see the waves unbridled force as it crashes against the dark beach.

Puffins and birdwatching: Several bird species, including puffins, call Reynisfjara home. Visitors may get the chance to see these endearing seabirds as they congregate on the cliffs close to the shore during the nesting season.

Jökulsárlón Glacier Lagoon

Jökulsárlón is a stunning glacial lagoon about 370 kilometres east of Reykjavik in southeast Iceland. By melting ice from the adjacent Breiamerkurjökull glacier, a surreal scene of floating icebergs is created, producing this magnificent natural beauty.

Iceberg Paradise: Jökulsárlón is well-known for its spectacular display of icebergs, which float peacefully in the lagoon's pure waters. A photographer's heaven, the icebergs are available in a variety of sizes and forms and come in beautiful colours of blue as well as pure white.

Boat Tours: Take into account going on an iceberg-strewn boat excursion to truly enjoy Jökulsárlón's splendour. These excursions provide a rare chance to go up close to the icebergs, hear the sound of the ice breaking, and learn from professional guides about the glacial ecosystem.

Wildlife Encounters: Jökulsárlón is a flourishing environment that draws a variety of species in addition to being a home for icebergs. A variety of bird species, such as Arctic terns and skuas, as well as seals relaxing on the icebergs or swimming in the lagoon, are to be seen.

Vatnajökull National Park

Vatnajökull National Park is a huge and diversified natural paradise in southeast Iceland that includes the biggest glacier in Europe. The park is a must-see location on the South Coast since it provides a broad variety of activities and scenery.

Vatnajökull Glaciers: The park's eponymous glacier, Vatnajökull, is a spectacular sight to see and spans an area of around 8,100 square kilometres. It is a remarkable experience to explore the glacier's extensive ice fields, ice caves, and ice tunnels. For those looking for excitement, there are guided glacier walks and ice cave explorations available.

Skaftafell Nature Reserve: The Vatnajökull National Park's Skaftafell Environment Reserve is a haven for hikers and environment enthusiasts. Glaciers, rivers, waterfalls, and valleys with lush greenery are just a few of the many landscapes found in the reserve. Several hiking paths are suitable for people of all fitness levels and provide an opportunity to see breathtaking panoramic vistas.

Svartifoss Waterfall: Located in Skaftafell Nature Reserve, Svartifoss, which translates to "Black Falls," is a stunning waterfall. Svartifoss is distinguished by its one-of-a-kind basalt column background that looks like a natural cathedral. The Svartifoss trek is worth the effort and passes through lovely scenery.

Glacier Lagoon outflow: The outflow of the glacier lagoon, which is situated near the southern boundary of Vatnajökull National Park, offers an additional chance to view the point where ice and seawater collide. You may watch icebergs as they travel from Jökulsárlón to Diamond Beach nearby, where they wash ashore and provide an amazing contrast with the dark sand.

A thrilling journey that immerses you in the untamed beauty and majesty of nature is exploring Iceland's south coast. Each place provides a distinctive experience, from the flowing waterfalls of Seljalandsfoss and Skógafoss to the surreal black sand beach of Reynisfjara, the captivating Jökulsárlón Glacier Lagoon, and the varied landscapes of Vatnajökull National Park. Get ready to be enchanted by the South Coast's alluring beauty and make lifelong memories.

THE WESTFJORDS

Iceland's Westfjords are a wild and isolated area that provides an off-the-beaten-path experience. The Westfjords are a refuge for nature lovers and explorers with their spectacular terrain, beautiful fjords, and rich wildlife. This chapter examines the Westfjords' best features, displaying its distinctive landmarks, quaint communities, and outdoor pursuits.

Overview of the Westfjords

The deep Safjarardjp fjord divides the Westfjords peninsula from the rest of Iceland in the northwest of the island nation. This area, famous for its imposing cliffs, high mountains, and twisting fjords, is a haven for individuals seeking seclusion and unspoiled natural beauty.

Remote Wilderness: The Westfjords are one of Iceland's least populous and frequented regions, making it the ideal location for those seeking to spend time in unspoiled nature. The area's untainted vistas and distinctive charm have been preserved because of its rough topography and little infrastructure.

Spectacular Fjords: the Westfjords are well known for their magnificent fjords, where towering mountains tumble into deep, narrow inlets. With charming settlements tucked away along the beaches and possibilities for spectacular drives and walks to explore the surrounding environment, each fjord has its distinct personality.

Abundant Wildlife: The Westfjords' isolation and pristine environment draw a variety of animals. The region is home to a wide variety of bird species, including puffins, guillemots, and arctic terns, which will please bird watchers. In the seas along the peninsula, you could also see seals, whales, and dolphins.

Dynjandi Waterfall

The magnificent Dynjandi waterfall, often known as "The Jewel of the Westfjords," is situated in the secluded Dynjandi Voguebay. It is one of Iceland's most spectacular waterfalls and the biggest in the Westfjords.

Cascade of Beauty: Dynjandi is a collection of cascades that together provide an astounding display of natural beauty. The main waterfall has a wide, fan-like form and drops around 100 metres, making for an impressive spectacle. Smaller waterfalls are created along the route as the water pours down the slope, adding to the scene's attractiveness.

Hiking to Dynjandi: Hiking to Dynjandi gives you the chance to experience the wilderness close up and become immersed in it. The route offers expansive views of the fjords while passing across little streams and through lovely scenery. As there are some steep spots on the trail, be ready for a moderate climb.

Hidden Gems: Although Dynjandi is the main attraction, other waterfalls, and cascades are also worth exploring. Spend some time discovering the lesser-known but equally compelling minor falls, such as Haestahjallafoss, Strompgljfrafoss, and Göngumannafoss.

Látrabjarg Bird Cliffs

The westernmost point of the Westfjords is home to the breathtaking cliff formation known as Látrabjarg. These cliffs, which may reach a height of 440 metres above sea level, are home to one of the world's greatest seabird colonies.

Bird Watching Paradise: Látrabjarg is a refuge for birdwatchers, providing unrivalled possibilities to see and capture images of a variety of seabirds up close. A dynamic and vibrant display may be seen during the breeding season thanks to the species that nest on the cliffs, including puffins, razorbills, guillemots, and fulmars.

Dramatic Landscapes: The cliffs of Látrabjarg are a sight to see, in addition to the birds. In contrast to the thundering waves and the limitless horizon, the towering cliffs, which were carved by the North Atlantic Ocean's unrelenting might, provide a striking background. It is a location where you may witness the magnificence of nature.

Safe and Responsive Visits: It's crucial to respect the delicate environment and the safety of the birds when visiting Látrabjarg. Avoid stepping too close to the unstable cliff edges and don't harm the bird nests. To protect the preservation of this natural gem, stick to the trails that have been designated and any rules or limits that have been put in place.

Rauðasandur Beach

The Red Sand Beach, also known as Rauðasandur, is a distinctive and inaccessible beach that can be found on the Westfjords' southern coast. Rauðasandur has brilliant reddish-orange sand, in contrast to the normal black sand beaches seen in other regions of Iceland, which stands out dramatically against the environment.

Colours of the Sand: Rauðasandur red sand, which gives the beach its characteristic colour, is made of volcanic minerals combined with crushed scallop shells. Sand colour varies with the sunlight and weather, making for a captivating and constantly-evolving display.

Peaceful and Isolated: Rauðasandur is a quiet beach that exudes a sense of serenity and isolation. A backdrop of untainted natural beauty is provided by the immensity of the environment, which has undulating dunes and towering mountains in the distance.

Coastal Walks: Enjoy a stroll down the shore while taking in the sea air and the sound of the waves gently lapping against the shore. View the variety of birds that inhabit the dunes while exploring them. A spot to get away from the outer world and reconnect with nature is Rauasandur.

Ísafjörður and Other Towns

The major town and administrative centre of the Westfjords is Ísafjörður and Other Towns. Ísafjörður and Other Towns has a lovely and lively environment with colourful homes, a scenic port, and a variety of facilities and cultural activities despite its distant position.

Cultural Delights: Discover the rich history and cultural legacy of Ísafjörður and

Other Towns by strolling through its winding lanes. Learn about the history of the area by visiting the Westfjords Heritage Museum, or perusing the local galleries for modern art. The town also has several cultural events and festivals throughout the year, giving visitors a chance to fully experience the community's culture.

Quaint Villages: Outside of Safjörur, the Westfjords are filled with little, quaint towns that are well worth a visit. Towns like Bolungarvk, Patreksfjörur, and Suureyri create a warm and friendly ambiance while providing a window into the daily life of the locals. Discover their quaint cafés and stores, and take in the peace of rural life.

Outdoor Activities & Wildlife

The Westfjords provide a variety of chances for outdoor recreation and animal viewing. There are many thrills to be enjoyed in this secluded area, from hiking and kayaking to animal watching and boat cruises.

Hiking & Nature Walks: The Westfjords are a hiking and nature lover's heaven, with a variety of paths winding through stunning scenery. You'll be rewarded with breathtaking vistas and a sense of pure wildness whether you decide to trek along the shoreline, explore the rocky landscape, or travel into the isolated valleys.

Wildlife Encounters: Both on land and in the surrounding waterways, the Westfjords are home to a wide variety of species. Join a boat excursion to see these magnificent animals as they travel through the fjords: seals, dolphins, and even whales. The chances to see different seabirds and migratory species in their native environment will excite birdwatchers.

Kayaking & Water Activities: Take a kayaking expedition to see the fjords and shoreline from a new angle. Discover secluded coves, paddle across placid waterways, and take in the area's wild beauty and rocky cliffs. Kayaking offers the possibility to explore inaccessible locations and forge closer ties with the natural world.

The Westfjords is a region known for its unspoiled wilderness, far-off beauty, and unique experiences. The Westfjords will make a lasting impression on your spirit, whether you find yourself mesmerised by the tumbling waterfalls, absorbed in the vivid bird colonies, or seeing the picturesque towns and villages. Get ready to explore this extraordinary area and connect with its breathtaking natural beauty.

NORTHERN LIGHTS & WINTER ACTIVITIES

The Northern Lights and a variety of exhilarating winter sports make Iceland's winter season a unique experience. The fascinating world of the Aurora Borealis, the thrilling pursuits of winter sports, the captivating ice caves and glacier excursions, and the distinctive Christmas customs that make Iceland a winter paradise are all covered in this chapter.

Chasing the Northern Lights

The Northern Lights, commonly referred to as the Aurora Borealis, are one of the most sought-after natural phenomena that paint the winter sky with vivid hues and otherworldly beauty. What you need to know before seeing this breathtaking show in Iceland is as follows:

Optimal Conditions: The ideal evenings to observe the Northern Lights are clear, dark, and free of light pollution. Longer evenings throughout the winter, from September to April, increase the likelihood of seeing the lights dancing across the sky. For the finest viewing possibilities, keep an eye on the aurora prediction and be ready to travel into the countryside.

Ideal Location: The Northern Lights may be viewed all around Iceland, although particular places are known for having the best conditions. Away from the city lights, the countryside offers a spotless background against which the lights may sparkle. The distant areas of the Westfjords, the Snaefellsnes Peninsula, and Thingvellir National Park are all well-known locations.

Guided Tours: Consider taking part in a guided tour of the Northern Lights, which will be overseen by trained guides who are familiar with the best viewing spots and local weather patterns. These excursions increase your chances of seeing the lights and provide you with important knowledge about the science and legends surrounding this natural occurrence.

Patience & Persistence: The Northern Lights are a natural occurrence that is impacted by solar activity and meteorological conditions, so seeing them is not assured. Be prepared to search for the lights across several nights, and keep in mind that persistence and patience are essential. Even if the lights don't show up, the trip itself might be something to remember.

Winter Activities & Sports

The winter months in Iceland are filled with exhilarating pursuits and sports that celebrate the snowy vistas and ice delights. Listed below are a few thrilling excursions you might do during your winter visit:

Snowmobiling: Get a rush from zipping over a snow-covered countryside at top speed. In many places in Iceland, guided snowmobile trips are offered, letting you experience the exciting adrenaline rush of this thrilling sport while exploring glaciers, mountains, and lonely wilderness areas.

Dog Sledding: Set out on a dog sledding expedition and let a pack of eager huskies tow you over the snowy landscape. With the help of this age-old form of transportation, you can connect with these wonderful animals and take in the serenity of the snowy landscapes while having an immersive experience.

Skiing and snowboarding: Skiers and snowboarders of all skill levels may practise their sports in Iceland's mountains and ski areas. There are slopes suitable for families as well as difficult backcountry terrain. Visitors may easily access the ski resorts close to Reykjavik, such as Bláfjöll and Skálafell.

Ice fishing: Try your hand at catching trout or Arctic char below the frozen surface of a lake or fjord by joining a guided ice fishing adventure. In this special and peaceful environment, knowledgeable guides will supply the equipment and instruct you on the tactics required to hook a fish.

Winter Hiking: Lace up your boots and go out on a winter trek to see the breathtaking landscapes of Iceland, which are covered in a white covering of snow. There are hiking choices for all ability levels, ranging from quick, picturesque strolls to multi-day hikes. The Skaftafell Nature Reserve paths and the trip to Reykjadalur Hot Springs are also well-liked itineraries.

Ice Caves & Glacier Hikes

Iceland's glaciers become an incredible world of ice tunnels and frozen wonders throughout the winter. Hiking across old glaciers and exploring these natural ice sculptures is a fascinating experience:

Exploring Ice Cave: Explore the fascinating ice caverns that form inside Iceland's glaciers. These mysterious caves have complex structures and transparent blue walls that give them an ethereal appearance. A thrilling and secure journey is guaranteed by the guided excursions that are offered to take you securely into these caverns.

Glacier Hiking: Walking on the huge, icy landscapes of Iceland's glaciers is possible by participating in a guided glacier trek. You'll set out on an exciting trek through the icy landscape while wearing crampons and other safety gear, taking in the breathtaking ice formations, deep crevasses, and expansive mountain views.

Safety First: First and foremost, safety should always come first. Only qualified guides should be used while exploring ice caves or trekking glaciers. For a safe and pleasurable experience, it is essential to have local knowledge and skills because glaciers are dynamic and possibly dangerous ecosystems. Be sure to adhere to your guide's recommendations, dress correctly, and be ready for rapidly changing weather conditions.

Icelandic Christmas customs

Icelandic Christmas customs are steeped in folklore and contribute to the winter's distinctive and magical mood. Here are several practices and traditions that give the holiday season a unique feel:

Yule Lads: Iceland's equivalent of Santa Claus is known as the Yule Lads. Children are visited by these thirteen naughty figures throughout the thirteen nights leading up to Christmas. Each Yule Lad has its own personality and places tokens of affection, such as potatoes, in the shoes of good-behaved kids.

Christmas Markets: Visit the festive Christmas markets hosted in several towns and cities, including Reykjavik and Akureyri. These markets provide a festive atmosphere with vendors offering handcrafted items, authentic Icelandic foods, and one-of-a-kind Christmas decorations. It's a great chance to get into the Christmas spirit and buy unusual presents.

Candle Lighting: On Christmas Eve, Icelanders engage in a custom known as "Jólabókaflóð," or the "Christmas Book Flood," in which families exchange books as gifts and the evening is spent curled up with a new book and a cup of hot cocoa.

Christmas Food: Specialties like smoked lamb, pickled herring, and leaf bread are common Christmas food in Iceland. On Christmas Eve, it's also usual to consume a celebratory lunch that often includes roast pig or pickled skate, followed by a selection of Christmas pastries and sweets.

New Year's Eve Fireworks: Icelanders enjoy a fantastic fireworks show on New Year's Eve. It has become customary to assemble with loved ones and friends to witness the vibrant fireworks that mark the beginning of the new year.

Winter in Iceland is a season of enchantment when the country's natural beauties and cultural traditions come together to offer visitors a genuinely wonderful experience. Iceland provides a winter trip unlike any other, with opportunities to hunt for the Northern Lights, participate in exhilarating winter sports, explore ice caves and glaciers, and embrace distinctive Christmas traditions. In this winter paradise, embrace the season and make amazing memories.

OFF THE BEATEN PATH

Iceland is well known for its stunning scenery and well-liked tourist attractions. For those looking for an adventure more off the beaten path, this chapter investigates remote and unknown locations, the thrilling adventure of hiking and camping in the Highlands, the distinctive allure of the Westman Islands, the geological wonders of the Reykjanes Peninsula, and the undiscovered gems along the West Coast.

Remote & Lesser Known Locations

Although the country's famous attractions draw big visitors, there are undiscovered regions of Iceland that provide peace and unspoiled beauty. Here are a few off-the-beaten-path places worth visiting:

Hornstrandir Nature Reserve: The Westfjords' Hornstrandir Nature Reserve is a pristine wilderness region renowned for its craggy cliffs, breathtaking fjords, and an abundance of animals. This secluded area, which can only be reached by boat, provides possibilities for trekking, birding, and seeing nature at its most unadulterated.

Húsavík's Surrounding Areas: Although Húsavík is regarded as the "Whale Watching Capital of Iceland," the region around it is home to pristine scenery and undiscovered treasures. Visit the lesser-known fishing communities along the coast, such as Raufarhöfn and Kópasker, or explore the neighbouring Sbyrgi Canyon, a horseshoe-shaped ravine flanked by high rocks.

Strandir Coastline: Located in the Westfjords, the Strandir Coastline is a rough and remote area distinguished by imposing cliffs, black sand beaches, and prehistoric legend. Discover unknown coves, stop at distant hot springs, and savour the ethereal environment of this less-visited region of Iceland.

Hiking & Camping in the Highlands

The Icelandic Highlands, with their vast, unspoiled natural areas and difficult terrain, provide a true wilderness experience. In the Highlands, hiking and camping offer a chance to experience the natural beauty of the surroundings. What you need to know is as follows:

Fjallabak Nature Reserve: The southern Highlands' Fjallabak Nature Reserve is home to many hiking paths that wind through surreal scenery. A well-known multi-day hike, the Laugavegur Trail, passes through a variety of landscapes, including colourful mountains, geothermal sites, and glacial valleys. In selected spots along the route, camping is permitted.

Askja Caldera: The Askja Caldera is a volcanic paradise with exotic scenery, and it is situated in the northern Highlands. To experience the bizarre surroundings, hike to the edge of the Vti Crater, a geothermal lake inside the caldera. Camping is permitted close by, so you can fully appreciate this distinctive setting.

Thórsmörk: A lush valley in the southern Highlands known for its breathtaking scenery and strenuous hiking paths, Thórsmörk is tucked between three glaciers. Explore the region on multi-day hikes like the Fimmvöruháls Trail, which leads you through stunning waterfalls, glacial rivers, and expansive views.

Preparation and Safety: Safety and preparedness are key while hiking and camping in the Highlands. You should be well-prepared and mindful of the difficult terrain. Plan your routes, let someone know where you're going, and pack the right outdoor gear, such as trustworthy hiking boots, warm clothes, and a good map or

GPS. Weather conditions can quickly change, so be aware and ready for anything.

Westman Islands

The Westman Islands (Vestmannaeyjar), which are off the coast of Iceland, are home to a diverse range of animals, rich history, and stunning natural scenery. The following are some reasons to visit the Westman Islands:

Heimaey: The biggest island in the archipelago, Heimaey, is home to the quaint village of Vestmannaeyjar, where you can visit the Eldheimar Museum to learn more about the island's volcanic past and the eruption of Eldfell in 1973. Visit puffin colonies, take a trek up the volcanic hills for panoramic views, and explore the charming port.

Eldfell Volcano: Exploring Eldfell, the volcano that erupted in 1973 and permanently altered the landscape, is a must-do on a trip to the Westman Islands. Hike to the top and be amazed by the lunar-like landscape to experience nature's power firsthand.

Encounters with Wildlife: The Westman Islands are well-known for their voluminous birdlife. Visit the archipelago by boat to see puffins, guillemots, and other seabirds that are breeding. In the vicinity's waterways, there's also a possibility to see orcas, seals, and whales.

Outdoor Activities: Explore the Westman Islands' rocky coastline by kayaking or taking a rib boat trip, which will allow you to pass through sea caves and get up close to the towering cliffs. The islands provide a variety of outdoor activities for all interests, including hiking, golfing, and fishing.

Reykjanes Peninsula

The Reykjanes Peninsula, a geologically active region with breathtaking scenery and distinctive attractions, is situated in the southwest of Iceland. On the Reykjanes Peninsula, you may explore the following:

The Blue Lagoon: Known for its milky-blue, mineral-rich waters, the Blue Lagoon is a well-known geothermal spa. Enjoy a revitalising mud mask, unwind in the warm geothermal pools, and take in the surreal surroundings. For those looking for leisure and natural beauty, the Blue Lagoon should be on their travel itinerary.

Bridge between Continents: The Mid-Atlantic Ridge, which separates the North American and Eurasian tectonic plates, is crossed by the Reykjanes Peninsula. Visit the Bridge Between Continents, a little footbridge that serves as a representation of the bond between the two continents. The view of the geological processes at play from the bridge is very interesting.

Krýsuvík Geothermal Area: Visit the bizarre landscapes of the Krýsuvík Geothermal Area, which are highlighted by boiling mud pots, steaming vents, and vibrant mineral deposits. Follow the indicated hiking paths to get a close-up view of this geothermal paradise and experience the unbridled force of the planet's geothermal activity.

Reykjanesviti Lighthouse: Visit the renowned Reykjanesviti Lighthouse, which is situated on the peninsula's southwest point. This antique lighthouse commands a commanding presence against the imposing cliffs of the shore and provides expansive views of the untamed coastline. Investigate the neighbourhood, which is renowned for its geological characteristics and birds.

Exploring the West Coast

The West Coast of Iceland is frequently disregarded by tourists despite having beautiful scenery and undiscovered treasures. The West Coast's highlights are as follows:

Snæfellsnes Peninsula: Often referred to as "Iceland in Miniature," the peninsula gives a condensed representation of the varied landscapes of the nation. Discover the gorgeous Kirkjufell Mountain, stop by the quaint fishing communities of Stykkishólmur and Grundarfjörur, and be amazed by the Snæfellsjökull volcano, which is said to be a sacred site.

Hraunfossar & Barnafoss Waterfalls: The waterfalls of Hraunfossar and Barnafoss, which are in western Iceland, are a hidden treasure that should be explored. While Barnafoss, which translates to "Children's Waterfall," is well-known for its churning waters and interesting legend,

Hraunfossar is a collection of waterfalls that appear to spill out of a lava field.

A sense of discovery and a chance to see lesser-known natural treasures are provided by exploring the secluded areas of Iceland's west coast. The West Coast provides a singular and off-the-beaten-path experience, whether it is the Snaefellsnes Peninsula, the mesmerising waterfalls, or the secret beaches.

As a whole, this section explores the fascination of Iceland's distant and less-visited locations, the thrilling adventure of trekking and camping in the Highlands, the allure of the Westman Islands, the geological activity of the Reykjanes Peninsula, and the undiscovered treasures along the West Coast. You will discover the untamed beauty and undiscovered gems that make Iceland such a unique travel destination by veering off the beaten path.

ICELANDIC CUISINES AND DINING

Iceland's culinary sector has developed recently and now offers a distinctive fusion of traditional Icelandic food and cutting-edge culinary pleasures. This chapter examines the wide variety of mouthwatering cuisines, both traditional and modern, that Iceland has to offer. Get ready for an extraordinary gastronomic trip with your taste senses!

Traditional Icelandic Dishes

Geographical features and the availability of natural resources have a significant impact on Icelandic cuisine. Some classic foods to try are listed below:

Plokkfiskur: A hearty meal created with boiling fish (often cod or haddock) and potatoes that have been combined with butter and milk. Typically, onions, salt, and pepper are used as seasonings.

Hangikjöt: In Iceland, smoked lamb is a well-liked delicacy. Traditionally eaten around Christmas time, hangikjöt is frequently served with potatoes, peas, and a rich béchamel sauce.

Rúgbrauð: A rye bread that is often baked in geothermal ovens, it is rich and black. It tastes somewhat sweet and goes nicely with smoked salmon or butter.

Harðfiskur: Also known as "Icelandic fish jerky," Harðfiskur is produced by crisping up fish, usually cod or haddock. It is a common snack that is frequently eaten with butter or as a side to soups.

Skyr: A milder-flavoured dairy product that is creamy and thick and resembles yoghourt. High in protein, skyr is frequently consumed with berries or in desserts.

Contemporary Icelandic Food

Iceland's culinary landscape has experienced a recent upsurge in originality and ingenuity. Chefs are using regional ingredients and fusing traditional tastes with cutting-edge cooking methods. Here are a few contemporary Icelandic meals you should try:

Grilled Langoustine: Iceland is well-known for its little lobsters known as langoustine. Popular cuisine that highlights the delicate and sweet flavour of this regional shellfish is grilled langoustine.

Salted Cod: Typically served as a main dish and is made by brining the fish first, then boiling or frying it. It is often served with potatoes, veggies, and a buttery sauce.

Lamb Fillet: The taste of Iceland's grass-fed lamb is unsurpassed. A must-try entrée is lamb fillet that has been grilled to perfection and is served with fresh seasonal veggies and mouth watering sauces.

Arctic Char: This regional fish, which is sourced locally, has a delicate flavour and is akin to salmon and trout. It is frequently grilled or pan-fried, served with a variety of sauces, and accompanied by new potatoes or veggies.

Skyr-based Desserts: From fruity Skyr parfaits to creamy Skyr cakes, skyr has gained popularity as a dessert component. Don't pass up the chance to enjoy these delectable and nutritious delicacies.

Unique Icelandic Ingredients

Unique and top-notch foods are more readily available in Iceland because of its pristine environment and sustainable methods. The following elements give Icelandic food a special flavour:

Icelandic Sea Salt: Icelandic sea salt is prized for its cleanliness and mineral richness and is gathered from the clear coastal waters of the nation. It may be bought as a memento and is used to season many different types of food.

Arctic Thyme: In the highlands of Iceland, this fragrant plant grows naturally. It is frequently used to season lamb or fish since it gives food a delicate, slightly spicy taste.

Berries: Crowberries, blueberries, and bilberries are just a few of the berries that may be found in Iceland. These wild berries are used to lend a burst of natural sweetness to sweets, jams, and sauces.

Reindeer: Although less prevalent than fish or lamb, reindeer is a distinctive element in Icelandic cooking. It may be found in conventional stews or grilled preparations and is frequently offered as a specialty dish in expensive restaurants.

Dining Experiences & Food Festivals

Explore the neighbourhood eating scene and go to food festivals to truly experience Iceland's gastronomic wonders. Particularly Reykjavik provides a thriving culinary scene with a variety of eateries, cafés, and pubs to satisfy every taste.

Food Festivals: Iceland holds many food festivals every year to honour regional cuisine and culinary customs. You may sample Icelandic cuisine during events like the Food and Fun Festival in Reykjavik and the Lobster Festival in Höfn, to name just a couple.

Farm-to-Table Dining: Organic and locally sourced products are frequently used in Icelandic restaurants. Discover farm-to-table eating options that showcase the great quality and freshness of Icelandic products.

Seafood Delicacies: As an island country, Iceland is well known for its seafood. Visit eateries that specialise in seafood to indulge in fresh Atlantic Ocean catches including langoustine, salmon, and Arctic char.

Icelandic Craft Beer: Enjoy a glass of Icelandic craft beer with your meals. The beer industry in the nation is expanding, with brewers providing distinctive and excellent beers motivated by regional ingredients.

Finally, Iceland provides a wonderful and varied food experience. There is something for every culinary enthusiast, from classic recipes that emphasise regional ingredients and traditions to cutting-edge reinterpretations that highlight creativity and innovation. Discover Iceland's traditional and contemporary cuisine, delight in unusual ingredients, and enjoy dining experiences and food festivals to fully appreciate how extraordinary Iceland's culinary landscape is. Bon appetit!

PRACTICAL INFORMATION

To ensure a smooth and pleasurable trip to a new place, it is crucial to be knowledgeable about practical details. This chapter concentrates on crucial information about money, tips, taxes, health and safety concerns, communication and internet access, helpful words, regional etiquette, and emergency contacts in Iceland.

Currency, Tipping, and Taxes

Currency: The Icelandic króna (ISK) is the country's official unit of exchange. Although credit cards are generally accepted across the nation, it is advisable to have extra cash on hand for smaller businesses or locations that might not take cards. Banks, authorised currency exchange offices, and airports all offer currency exchange services.

Tipping: Tipping is uncommon in Iceland since services are frequently already included in the bill. However, you could decide to give a little tip as a sign of gratitude if you experience great service.

Taxes: Value-added tax (VAT) is a tax that is applied to the purchase of goods and services in Iceland. Icelandic people who don't live there can get their VAT back on some goods. You must obtain a tax-free form at the time of purchase and produce it at the VAT refund counter at the airport before departure to get the refund.

Health and Safety

Medical Facilities: The grade of medical treatment in Iceland is quite excellent, and emergency services are readily available. Call 112 for assistance if a medical emergency arises. Major towns and cities have hospitals and clinics as well as other medical services. Before visiting Iceland, it is important to purchase travel insurance that includes medical coverage.

Safety Precautions: Generally speaking, Iceland is a safe nation with low crime rates. However, it's crucial to use common sense safety measures, such as protecting your possessions, securing your car, and paying attention to your surroundings, especially in busy places or at tourist sites. When indulging in outdoor activities, it's also a good idea to heed instructions and caution about natural risks, such as glacier safety or environmental conditions.

Communication & Internet Access

Communication: Iceland has a well-developed telecommunications infrastructure and mobile phone coverage is typically great, especially in outlying locations. The majority of mobile networks provide international roaming services, although it is advised to verify with your service provider about coverage and costs before departing. You may get a local SIM card in a variety of places, such as airports and convenience stores if you wish to use one.

Internet Access: Free Wi-Fi is freely accessible in many hotels, cafés, restaurants, and open areas around Iceland. Additionally, public libraries and Wi-Fi hotspots have access to the internet. Consider renting a portable Wi-Fi gadget or utilising a local SIM card with a data package if you need consistent access.

Useful Phrases and Local Etiquette

Useful Phrases: Even though many Icelanders are competent in English, knowing a few fundamental Icelandic words and phrases will improve your trip and demonstrate that you value the local tongue. These words and phrases are helpful:

- ❖ Hello: Hallo
- ❖ Thank You: Takk
- ❖ Please: Vinsamlegast.
- ❖ Excuse me: Afsakið

- ❖ Yes: Já
- ❖ No: Nei
- ❖ Goodbye: Bless
- ❖ Vinur: Friend
- ❖ Kaffi: Coffee
- ❖ Gluggaveður: Weather that is nice to look at but not so pleasant to be in
- ❖ Skál: Cheers
- ❖ Góðan dag: Good day
- ❖ Bókasafn: Library

Local Etiquette: Icelanders place high importance on decency, respect, and private space. It's polite to shake hands and make eye contact with someone when you first meet them. It is customary to take off your shoes while entering a person's home or various places, such as guesthouses. Furthermore, it's crucial to stick to approved routes and respect the environment because Iceland contains fragile ecosystems that need to be preserved.

Emergency Contacts

Emergency Services: To contact Iceland's emergency services in an emergency, dial 112. For medical emergencies, fire help, and police support, dial this number.

Consular Assistance: Contact your respective embassy or consulate in Iceland if you need consular assistance with anything, including lost passports or other related problems. They can offer direction and assistance in these circumstances.

You can travel the nation with confidence and ease if you are aware of the local etiquette regarding money, tipping, taxes, health and safety issues, communication alternatives, and internet access. You may completely immerse yourself in the Icelandic experience while guaranteeing your health and safety at all times by being well-prepared and knowledgeable.

TRAVEL TIPS AND RESOURCES

To make the most of your trip, extensive planning and preparation are required while visiting Iceland. This chapter offers helpful information and travel advice that will improve your time in Iceland. It includes suggestions on taking better photos, useful websites and applications, books and movies to watch, and sustainable travel methods.

Financial Advice

Travel During the Shoulder Seasons: Spring and fall are the best times to go to Iceland since the weather is still nice and there aren't as many people around. These times of year are often less expensive for lodging and travel.

Plan Your Meals: Make a food plan because eating out in Iceland can be pricey.

Consider self-catering to cut costs by reserving lodgings with kitchens and shopping at large-format stores. Additionally, choose lunch specials at restaurants, which are frequently less expensive than supper selections, or sample the local street cuisine.

Explore free attractions and activities: There are many free natural beauties to explore in Iceland. Take advantage of the free hiking paths, hot springs, waterfalls, and magnificent overlooks that are available. Plan your agenda with these cost-free activities in mind after doing some research.

Rent a Car & Share Expenses: By having a car, you may travel independently around Iceland and reach outlying locations. Consider splitting the cost of renting a car and petrol if you're going with a group to make it more affordable than using solo transportation.

Photography Advice

Pack the Right Gear: Iceland's breathtaking scenery offers numerous picture possibilities. To photograph the picturesque panoramas, waterfalls, and captivating Northern Lights, be sure to pack a reliable tripod, wide-angle lens, and polarising filter. To guarantee you don't miss a shot, bring multiple memory cards and batteries.

Be Prepared for the Weather: Since Icelandic weather is erratic, it's crucial to have the proper protective clothing for your photography equipment. To protect your equipment from rain or spray close to waterfalls and other wet areas, invest in a waterproof camera bag or use a rain cover.

Capture the Unique Light: Iceland is renowned for its constantly shifting lighting, particularly during the golden hours. Stay out late to photograph the brilliant hues of the sunset or get up early to capture the calm morning light. Utilise various setups and exposures to your advantage to capture the alluring Icelandic light.

Respect the environment: It's essential to put sustainability and moral behaviour first when shooting Iceland's delicate scenery. Avoid trampled vegetation by remaining on designated routes. Observe any signs designating forbidden zones. To prevent upsetting or harming wildlife, keep your distance and be observant of your surroundings.

Useful Websites and Apps

Inspired by Iceland (www.inspiredbyiceland.com): The official tourist website of Iceland, offers thorough details on destinations, activities, lodgings, and travel advice.

Vedur (www.vedur.is): The Icelandic Meteorological Office's website provides up-to-date weather predictions, information on traffic, and other crucial weather-related details.

Appy Hour (www.appyhour.is): Use this app to find Reykjavik's many pubs and restaurants happy hours and drink specials so you may have a drink at a lower cost.

112 Iceland (www.112.is): This mobile app provides Emergency services, safety advice, and the opportunity to share your position with first responders.

Sustainable Travel Practices

Respect Nature and Wildlife: Respect the environment and animals by taking your waste with you, sticking it on designated pathways, and minimising the disturbance of wildlife and plants. Ensure that future generations can continue to enjoy Iceland's beautiful nature.

Conserve Water and Energy: Iceland's natural resources should be preserved since they are valuable. Water can be scarce in some isolated regions, so use it cautiously there. Choose lodgings with energy-efficient heating and lighting systems and other sustainable practices.

Support regional enterprises and communities: By booking with locally run hotels, eateries, and tour companies to support the regional economy. To support local artists and craftspeople, buy locally manufactured goods and trinkets.

Use Environmentally Friendly Transportation: When touring cities and towns, think about taking public transit, cycling, or walking. When feasible, carpool and use fuel-efficient or electric cars when renting a car.

Offset your carbon footprint: Take into account reducing your carbon emissions by assisting programs that provide verified carbon offsets and promote environmental causes. Numerous businesses provide carbon offset programs to lessen the effect of your vacation.

You'll have a more fun and responsible voyage by putting money-saving tactics into practice, adhering to photographic advice, employing practical websites and applications, and engaging in sustainable travel. For a memorable and sustainable journey, embrace Iceland's beauty while protecting its ecosystem and helping local people.

CONCLUSION

The "Iceland Travel Guide 2023" is your comprehensive travel companion as you discover Iceland's breathtaking landscapes, rich history, lively culture, and one-of-a-kind experiences. Whether you're a lover of the outdoors, a thrill-seeker, or a cultural traveller, this book gives you the information and insights you need to make the most of your trip.

This guide takes you on a virtual tour of Iceland's spectacular locations, from the busy streets of Reykjavik to the isolated Westfjords, from the famous Golden Circle to the stunning South Coast. It offers helpful advice on organising your trip, such as the ideal time to travel, visa requirements, travel alternatives, and lodging possibilities.

Discover old sagas, visit top-notch museums, and savour regional cuisine as you immerse yourself in Iceland's intriguing history and lively culture. Go on glacier walks, chase the Northern Lights for the thrill of it, and behold the might of falling waterfalls.

This travel guide ventures beyond the well-known sights, leading you off the beaten track to unexplored locales. As a result, you may take advantage of Iceland's beauty while protecting its natural beauty for future generations. It also offers insights into sustainable tourism habits.

The "Iceland Travel Guide 2023" is your dependable travel companion whether you're looking for heart-pounding activities, serene natural experiences, or cultural immersion. It provides thorough details, expert advice, and suggested resources to assist you in designing a unique and exciting adventure across the region of fire and ice.

Pack your luggage, explore Iceland's charm, and let the "Iceland Travel Guide 2023" serve as your road map for a memorable trip. Prepare to make lasting memories as you learn why tourists from all over the world continue to be enthralled by Iceland.

APPENDIX

You will find more tools to help you plan and navigate your trip in the appendix part of our Iceland travel guide. A dictionary of Icelandic vocabulary will help you get more familiar with the local language, example itineraries will help you organise your time, maps and navigation advice will help you make sure you don't miss any important locations, and suggestions for tours and excursions will help you get the most out of your time in Iceland.

Sample Itineraries

Here are two sample itineraries that highlight various facets of Iceland so that you may make the most of your time there:

Classic Ring Road Adventure (10 days):

Day 1-2: Tour Reykjavik and the Golden Circle Route, taking in sights including Gullfoss Waterfall, Geysir Geothermal Area, and Þingvellir National Park.

Day 3-4: Visit Seljalandsfoss Waterfall, Skógafoss Waterfall, Reynisfjara Black Sand Beach, and Jökulsárlón Glacier Lagoon on days three and four of your journey down the South Coast.

Day 5-6: Explore the East Fjords, taking in the gorgeous fishing villages, hiking paths, and tranquillity of the area.

Day 7-8: Travel to Lake Mývatn in the north, which is renowned for its geothermal activity and breathtaking scenery. Go whale watching in Húsavík and the Mývatn Nature Baths.

Day 9-10: Tour the Snaefellsnes Peninsula, which is renowned for its stunning coastline, Snfellsjökull Glacier, and quaint settlements. Return to Reykjavik to catch your flight.

Off-the-Beaten-Path Adventure (7 days)

Day 1-2: Start in Reykjavik and take in the thriving food scene, museums, and cultural landmarks of the city.

Day 3: Travel to the Westfjords, where you may see the spectacular landscapes, Dynjandi Waterfall, Látrabjarg Bird Cliffs, and more.

Day 4: Visit the Snæfellsnes Peninsula. It is renowned for its varied scenery, which includes volcanic peaks, black-sand beaches, and Kirkjufell Mountain.

Day 5-6: Go on a multi-day trekking and camping excursion in the secluded Highlands. Find out about secret valleys, vibrant mountains, and hot springs.

Day 7: Travel back to Reykjavik, stopping en route to unwind in geothermal baths or browse local boutiques and art galleries.

Note: These suggested itineraries can be modified based on your interests, free time, and preferred modes of transportation.

Maps and Navigation

For a successful journey in Iceland, it's essential to have accurate maps and to know your alternatives for getting about. Here are some helpful resources for you:

Road Map: Get a thorough road map of Iceland to help you find your way through the nation's motorways, roads, and attractions. These maps can be obtained via bookstores, visitor information centres, or mobile applications.

GPS navigation: Think about bringing your own GPS gadget or hiring a car with one. This will make it easier for you to navigate Iceland's roadways and guarantee that you get where you're going.

Mobile Apps: Use smartphone applications for real-time navigation, such as Google Maps, Maps. me, or Waze. Be sure to download offline maps in case you come across places with spotty internet.

Signage: Road signs should not be ignored because they are well-marked and obvious in Iceland. Observe the posted speed restrictions and any further directions.

Recommended Tours & Excursions

Booking guided tours and excursions will help you get the most out of your trip to

Iceland and provide you access to exclusive experiences. Popular choices comprise:

Glacier Hiking and Ice Cave Tours: Explore the breathtaking ice formations and caverns within Iceland's glaciers with the help of knowledgeable guides on glacier hiking and ice cave excursions.

Puffin and Whale Watching Tours: Take a boat journey to see Iceland's diverse wildlife, including puffins and several whale species, on a puffin and whale-watching cruise.

ATV or Super Jeep Tours: Take a thrilling trip over rocky terrain, volcanic landscapes, and far-flung regions of the nation on an ATV or Super Jeep.

Horseback Riding Tours: Discover Iceland's distinctive horse breed, the Icelandic horse, while travelling across beautiful terrain on horseback.

Northern Lights Tours: Join a nighttime journey to search for the captivating Northern Lights in prime viewing areas free from light pollution.

These tours can be scheduled through regional travel agencies or internet resources. To have a safe and enjoyable trip, make sure you select reliable operators with skilled guides.

Finally, our Iceland travel guide's appendix section offers extra resources to make your vacation even better. Sample itineraries help you organise your time, maps and navigational advice guarantee you don't miss important locations, an Icelandic language dictionary facilitates conversation, and suggested tours and excursions provide memorable experiences. Use these tools to personalise your trip and maximise your time in Iceland.